Thrill Me

The Leopold & Loeb Story

A musical

Book, music and lyrics by
Stephen Dolginoff

Samuel French — London
www.samuelfrench-london.co.uk

THRILL ME:
THE LEOPOLD & LOEB STORY

First produced by Jim Kierstead as part of the Fourth Annual Midtown International Theatre Festival at the Abingdon Theatre Arts Complex in New York, on July 16, 2003, with the following cast:

Nathan Leopold	Christopher Totten
Richard Loeb	Matthew S. Morris

Voices: Sarah Crowley, Archie T. Tridmorten and Sean Kenin

Directed by Martin Charnin
Lighting design by Thom Weaver
Musical direction by Gabriel Kahane
Production stage managed by Amy M. Epstein

Subsequently produced Off-Broadway in New York at the York Theatre Company (James Morgan, Producing Artistic Director) in association with Jim Kierstead, opening on May 26, 2005, with the following cast:

Nathan Leopold	Matt Bauer*
Richard Loeb	Doug Kreeger**

Voices: John McMartin, Stephen Bogardus and Michael Rupert

*Stephen Dolginoff took over the role of Nathan Leopold on June 27th, 2005
**Shonn Wiley took over the role of Richard Loeb on August 1st, 2005

Directed by Michael Rupert
Designed by James Morgan
Musical direction by Eugene Gwozdz
Lighting design by Thom Weaver

Costume design by Jennifer Paar
Sound design by Joey Morano
Production stage managed by Scott F. Delacruz

Subsequently produced in London by Climar
Productions at the Tristan Bates Theatre, opening on
April 5, 2011, before moving to the Charing Cross
Theatre and opening on May 17 2011 in a version
produced by Climar Productions in association with
Philip Abel, Jim Kierstead and the Charing Cross
Theatre, with the following cast:

Nathan Leopold	Jye Frasca
Richard Loeb	George Maguire

Voices: Lee Mead, Patricia Quinn and Les Dennis

Directed by Guy Retallack
Musical direction by David Keefe
Designed by James Turner
Lighting design by Richard Williamson
Production stage managed by Anjali Kale

CHARACTERS

Nathan Leopold, 19 (also plays Nathan at 53)
Richard Loeb, 19

Voices (pre-recorded): The parole board (2 voices), Radio Newscaster

SYNOPSIS OF SCENES

PROLOGUE A parole board hearing room at Joliet Prison
SCENE 1 Jackson Park, Chicago
SCENE 2 In front of the warehouse
SCENE 3 Richard's bedroom
SCENE 4 Nathan's bedroom
SCENE 5 The parole board hearing room
SCENE 6 Nathan's bedroom
SCENE 7 Richard's garage/the parole board hearing room
SCENE 8 Near a school yard
SCENE 9 The woods near Wolf Lake
SCENE 10 Richard's bedroom
SCENE 11 Nathan's house/Richard's house
SCENE 12 The parole board hearing room
SCENE 13 Nathan's bedroom
SCENE 14 Jackson Park
SCENE 15 A police interrogation room
SCENE 16 Richard's jail cell
SCENE 17 The back of a prison transportation wagon
SCENE 18 The parole board hearing room

Time — 1924/1958

MUSICAL NUMBERS

No. 1	**Prelude**	
No. 2	**Why**	Nathan
No. 3	**Everybody Wants Richard**	Nathan
No. 4	**Tag: Everybody Wants Richard**	Nathan
No. 5	**Nothing Like A Fire**	Richard and Nathan
No. 6	**A Written Contract (Part 1)**	Richard and Nathan
No. 7	**A Written Contract (Part 2)**	Richard
No. 8	**A Written Contract (Part 3)**	Richard and Nathan
No. 9	**A Written Contract (Part 4)**	Richard and Nathan
No. 10	**Thrill Me**	Nathan and Richard
No. 11	**The Plan**	Richard and Nathan
No. 12	**Way Too Far**	Nathan
No. 13	**Roadster**	Richard
No. 14	**Superior**	Nathan and Richard
No. 15	**Ransom Note**	Richard and Nathan
No. 16	**My Glasses/Just Lay Low**	Nathan and Richard
No. 17	**I'm Trying To Think**	Richard and Nathan
No. 18	**Way Too Far** reprise	Nathan
No. 19	**Keep Your Deal With Me**	Richard and Nathan
No. 20	**Afraid**	Richard
No. 21	**Life Plus Ninety-nine Years**	Nathan and Richard
No. 22	**Finale: Thrill Me**	Nathan
No. 23	**Bows/Exit Music**	

The piano score and vocal book are available on hire from Samuel French Ltd

BILLING REQUIREMENT

Any production of *Thrill Me: The Leopold & Loeb Story* must include the following credits on the title page in all programmes distributed:

Originally produced in New York City by Jim Kierstead

Off-Broadway production by The York Theatre Company
(James Morgan, Producing Artistic Director)

New York Cast Album available at www.thrillmethemusical.com

AUTHOR'S FOREWORD

I was originally inspired to write about Leopold and Loeb because I saw it as an opportunity to tell a very unusual love story. And thus *Thrill Me* is a dramatic musical about a relationship, not about a murder. The murder is part of the plot of course, but it is not the main focus. The dynamics of the relationship and its twists, turns, manipulations, shifts of power and ultimate surprise conclusion create the true drama and most compelling aspects of the show.

Performed with no intermission, with almost continuous musical underscore and no applause breaks, *Thrill Me* is conceived as a taut and unencumbered theatrical experience.

"Relationships can be murder" was the tag-line in the advertising for the Off-Broadway production. This helped emphasize that there is a small but definite amount of dark humour in the script and lyrics. Sometimes people will laugh at certain moments, sometimes they won't. But since the subject matter is very intense, a little release now and then can help the audience deal with the tension.

The characters are more complex than they appear. Nathan may seem needy at first, but he knows exactly what he wants and exactly how to get it. And what he obviously wants is Richard. Richard may treat Nathan badly on the surface, but he truly needs him and finds him appealing (though he may find it hard to admit), or else he could use someone else who worships him as his partner in crime. Remember, they are intellectual equals and have a long history together. It is important that the actors appear youthful, but it is not absolutely necessary to actually cast 19-year-olds in these very demanding roles. Regardless of their age, there should be a distinct physical contrast between the two.

To help accentuate the almost claustrophobic feeling of being trapped in a room with Leopold and Loeb, the parole board and radio voices must be pre-recorded or performed completely offstage. They are never to be portrayed by live actors seen by the audience.

Thrill Me is essentially Nathan's story, taking place in his memory as he tells the facts to the parole board. So he must never completely leave the stage except perhaps for a few seconds before *Superior* (to represent the murder being committed). This can easily be accomplished with a very fluid, abstract staging concept. Also, Nathan must never have to move set pieces or strike props at the end of a scene or before his lines to the parole board — Richard should always take care of this. It is also possible to simply hide the props around the set so they never have to be taken very far.

It is very important to help ensure there are no applause breaks by also having no complete black-outs. And to make crystal clear that Nathan is speaking to the parole board between scenes (and not merely to the audience) the parole board lighting should be extremely specific and recognizable.

When it comes time for Nathan to put his prison uniform back on for the last scene (the only time feasible for him to wear it again), it should be a quick and simple move, contingent upon easy access to where he left it after the prologue.

Simplicity is the key to *Thrill Me*. Nothing should interrupt the flow at any time. There should not be too much stage time spent taking off jackets, putting on hats, hanging up coats, moving around set pieces or doing major business with extra added things that aren't truly needed. There should be minimal props, only what is absolutely necessary, and they should be period authentic to the last detail. In 1924 cigarettes didn't have filters, car keys were very different looking, Zippo flip-top lighters hadn't been invented, candlestick telephones were still being used, etc.

Pace is also important. Erring on the side of playing it a little too slow is preferable to playing it a little too fast. The show should ideally run 85 minutes but at least be somewhere between 80-90 minutes. Any shorter and it is being performed too quickly.

Not much scenery is required for *Thrill Me*. It was presented in a tiny black box theatre in its original fringe festival presentation. The audience was on three sides and the set comprised six black cubes, which were never moved. The actors sat, climbed, typed, and set props on these cubes.

The Off-Broadway production was more elaborate, and whilst abstract, it had the utilitarian look of an abandoned warehouse. It featured a proscenium of dusty industrial windows, a shiny black floor, a few strategically-placed battered grey wooden crates of different sizes which were used as a desk, chairs and a bench; and three tall, black-tiled columns upstage in front of a black backdrop. Entrances and exits were often made from between these columns, which had prop storage behind them (and were lit from behind and between to stunning effect). The lighting design included the liberal use of a haze/fog machine to add drama and atmosphere to the noir-ish lighting plot (and create the feeling of a "memory" play) and there was a dramatic headlight effect for the *Roadster* song.

The South Korean version of *Thrill Me* was a far more extravagant affair with detailed platforms to represent each character's home, a huge, heavy "garage door" to open with deafening sound to reveal the headlights of Richard's Roadster behind it, a creepy illuminated walking footprint effect to represent the steps of the murder victim, and projected film of storm clouds swirling across the stage during the telephone song, to symbolize the passage of time.

The London production used a conceptual grid design at the back of the stage that resembled a large prison cell with movable pieces of furniture and props within its various sections.

The original costume design was very specific and revealing for each character. Each actor had one costume with additional pieces. Nathan wore dark colors in an old-fashioned style that was already out of date by 1924. His hair was parted in the middle and slicked back severely, which made him look more like his father than a teenager. On the other hand, Richard wore light, airy colours in the latest cuts and styles and a far more modern (for 1924) hairstyle. Nathan's prison uniform comprised a grey top with large buttons so he could get out of it quickly. He also wore a matching cap with a brim, which hid his hair and cast shadows on to his face to help create the illusion of an older man.

I have been asked if all of the plot developments in *Thrill Me* are based on fact. I confess to using dramatic licence to help make the material "sing." And I compressed some events so the story could unfold with only two characters. But every detail is at least inspired by actual events and facts. Did Nathan really drop his glasses on purpose or was it an accident? Can anyone say for sure? Those glasses were definitely what led to their capture. It is important to remember that we only know what they chose to tell the police, reporters, doctors and lawyers in 1924 and after. No one was there when Nathan and Richard were behind closed doors. No one was in their minds. No one knows what really happened between the two of them, and that is what *Thrill Me* explores and hypothesizes.

Stephen Dolginoff, 2011

ACKNOWLEDGMENTS

Heartfelt thanks to the following individuals
for their support and assistance in the development of
Thrill Me: The Leopold & Loeb Story
from New York to South Korea to London:

Jim Kierstead, Susan Dolginoff, Betty and Harold Levitt, Melinda Berk,
Camille Diamond, Eugene Gwozdz, Jim Morgan, Doug Kreeger,
Shonn Wiley, Seth Arrobas, Michael Park, Rob Harris
and Ron Gwiazda

A parole board hearing room at Joliet Prison. 1958

No. 1 Prelude

Prelude music begins

The Lights slowly fade up on a black, abstract set comprised of cubes, crates, platforms or other basic, multi-use pieces. This set will remain unchanged throughout with lighting used to indicate the many locales

The dark, shadowy figure of a 53-year-old man wearing a prison uniform and cap comes into view. It is Nathan Leopold, who is portrayed for the majority of the play as a young man. Thus through meticulous lighting, and with a careful gesture, stance, tilt of the head, deepening of voice, etc. this young actor embodies the older version of the character without altering his general appearance

Nathan addresses an unseen parole board, represented by disembodied (recorded) voices

Nathan I suppose you'd like me to sit down?

No response. He sits

Parole Board Voice 1 We can begin.

The strike of a gavel is heard

For the record: March thirteenth, nineteen fifty-eight, Joliet Prison, hearing A-nine-three-o-six-D-five. Nathan Leopold's fifth appearance before this parole board.

Nathan (*trying to make a joke*) They say the fifth time's the charm.

Silence

You want the facts again.

Parole Board Voice 2 We already know the facts about the crime you and Richard Loeb committed, from the transcripts, the reports ...

Parole Board Voice 1 From the newspapers ...

Parole Board Voice 2 The question is, do we have the truth? Do we know everything?

Nathan I've been here thirty-four years being punished for what I did as a kid. That's the truth.

Parole Board Voice 1 Your punishment was a gift. Thanks to your well-paid, publicity-hungry Clarence Darrow. Your life was spared ——

Parole Board Voice 2 (*interrupting*) He was hardly a kid at nineteen. He committed the crime of the century.

Nathan The papers just called it that to sell papers. Far worse crimes had been committed before. And since.

Parole Board Voice 1 Every crime has a reason. Sometimes a logical one, sometimes not, but still a reason. It seems you committed your crime for nothing but the thrill.

Nathan What is it you want?

Music begins

Parole Board Voice 2 What you've never told us. We want to know *why*.

Nathan Why ...

No. 2 Why

(*Singing*)   I'm sorry if I stumble ...
Though I'm tense ... I'll try
To give you what you're after ...
Tell you more.
I went along with Richard!
That's the reason why
They put me here
In nineteen twenty-four.
It was a child who killed
A child back then,
An old man still pays for that crime.

And I ask to be set free now.
Won't you try to see
That no one would be hurt
After all this time?

As I've said so often before!

But you've asked a simple question
And I've told you why.

> It wasn't on a dare or on a whim
> It's hard to comprehend now
> That the reason why
> Is simply:
> That I went along with him ...

The music continues

(*Speaking*) Richard and I were very close — from the beginning. We did everything together. Everything. We both graduated high school at the same time. We were fifteen-and-a-half! Then we went to the same college. But in the middle of our senior year he transferred to Michigan without telling me. It was a game he always liked to play to humiliate me. He'd stand me up, leave me stranded places, go away on a summer vacation without saying goodbye. Things like that. But after graduation, he came back to Chicago ...

The music gains momentum. Nathan stands and removes his prison uniform and cap, revealing his 1920s costume (and youthful hair) underneath. The Lights begin to become brighter ...

SCENE 1

Jackson Park. 1924

Nathan adjusts his stance as brighter lights reveal him to be an average, bookish 19-year-old of the early 1920s, waiting in the park

He checks his pocket-watch and is annoyed by the late hour. To keep himself busy, he puts a pair of binoculars to his eyes and spots a far away bird. He focuses on it intently

From behind, Richard Loeb, a darkly handsome, dapper, young man of 19 enters. He slowly approaches Nathan like a predator stalking his prey, and purposefully startles him

Richard Quit watching the stupid birds!

Nathan jumps out of his skin, but then turns to see Richard and relaxes. The music fades out

Nathan Bastard!

Nathan hugs Richard. Richard remains stiff

I was afraid you weren't going to show. I said three o'clock, didn't I?
Richard (*unemotional*) Hello, Nathan.
Nathan I've missed you.
Richard I know.
Nathan How have you been?
Richard Excellent.

Nathan puts his binoculars away

Nathan How does it feel to be a college graduate? You look ——
Richard Smarter?
Nathan — older!
Richard (*mocking*) It's only been six months, but I see you made it through those dark, atrocious, empty days ...
Nathan Shut up. I wish you'd gotten into Harvard Law school like me.
Richard How did you know I didn't?
Nathan John.
Richard John? My pea-brained brother? John is not only a snitch but a little bastard. I'm extremely happy with the University of Chicago, Nathan.
Nathan I'm glad *you're* happy. (*He puts his hand on Richard's shoulder*) Now, how about we do a little catching up?
Richard No. I've got a date. (*He pushes Nathan's hand off*)
Nathan A date?
Richard With my Nietzsche study group.
Nathan Nietzsche? When did you become interested in philosophy?
Richard Since I discovered I am a text book Superman.
Nathan But we haven't seen each other since you transferred.
Richard Nathan, why do you *think* I transferred?
Nathan I have no idea. I've had to get all my information from John and my bribery fund ran low.
Richard I'm sure a genius like you figured it out for yourself.

Nathan reluctantly nods

I've gotta go now. Unlike you, there are other people I like to spend time with.
Nathan I don't care about those other people.
Richard Good for you.
Nathan Because I know they don't mean anything to you.
Richard (*moving to leave*) And neither do you. Now, goodbye.

Nathan blocks his path

Auf wiedersehen.

Nathan moves to block him again

Move! (*He pushes Nathan away*) The others aren't so fucking annoying!

Music begins to creep in

Nathan I didn't think I annoyed you. I thought we had something different.
Richard (*mocking him*) "We have something different"!?

Nathan desperately sings

No. 3 Everybody Wants Richard

Nathan

Tell me, who can you have conversations with?
Share your twisted observations with?
Who else has a roughly similar view,
If not me?

You've played around with lots of losers
Who ended up as cheats and users
But who's been on the sidelines
Waiting for you,
If not me?

Oh, I've come to find
Ev'rybody wants Richard!
But they don't know
Your mind
The way that I do!
I see straight through
Anyone who needs Richard
They make
Me sick
They're good for just a kick!
They won't stick
The way that I do!

Richard (*coldly*) Have you got a light? (*He pulls out a cigarette case*)

Nathan's intensity grows

Nathan   When you cut off all our contact
                     How it hurt.
                     But I know you like to make me
                     Feel like dirt.
                     Now you're back and you know I'm beside you.
                     Your oldest, closest friend,
                     Who's sick of being lied to!

                     Tell me, who's the girl in which sorority?
                     I got word on good authority.
                     How can you assume she's worthy of you?
                     She's not me!

                     And I know there were sev'ral others.
                     According to your frat house brothers!
                     I even heard you passed around one or two!
                     Not with me!
                     Oh, your moves are fast!
                     Ev'rybody wants Richard
                     But they don't know your past
                     The way that I do.

Richard puts his cigarette in his mouth. Nathan pulls out a lighter and like a slave to his master, lights Richard's cigarette and watches him blow a stream of smoke

                     And God knows why I think you're so appealing
                     Or why you're always double crossing,
                     Double dealing!
                     But I rest my case —
                     I'm the one who needs Richard!
                     It's been too long
                     I've tried to be so strong
                     The others are wrong, they don't have a clue
                     Or know the real you!
                     Yes everybody wants Richard
                     But not
                     The way that I do!
                     Admit that you've missed me too!

Music continues under. Note: there is no applause break here or after any song until the very end

Richard I've only missed the worship. But, I guess I could change my plans and spend the evening with you ——
Nathan That's great ... we could go for a ride around the new ——
Richard — I could use your help.
Nathan What?
Richard That old abandoned warehouse off Dearborn ... the one we used to meet in before college?
Nathan Yeah, so?
Richard Is it still empty?
Nathan I think.
Richard Perfect. We're gonna make like Mrs O'Leary's cow!
Nathan Richard, not another fire!
Richard Hey, if you don't want to be with me ...

Richard starts to move away. Nathan quickly stops him

Nathan All right. But I'm just gonna stand guard like I used to.
Richard Eight o'clock. The warehouse. Now you'd better get busy. You've got to get the gasoline, buy some extra long matches, collect some old rags ...
Nathan All right, I'll meet you. Eight o'clock.

Richard moves to leave, but turns to Nathan and surprises him with a hard kiss on the lips

Richard There. Are you happy now?
Nathan (*almost embarrassed*) Yes.
Richard Eight o'clock. And *don't be late*.

Richard exits

Nathan watches him go and then sings to himself

No. 4 Tag: Everybody Wants Richard

Nathan
    It's been too long!
    I've tried to be so strong.
    The others are wrong,
    They don't have a clue
    Or know the real you.

Yes, everybody wants Richard
But not the way that I do!

The Lights instantly change to reflect the distinct look of the parole hearing in 1958. Nathan speaks to the board

I met him at the warehouse that night. Richard got so excited when he started the fire ... we used "Diamond Matches" — they always lit on the first strike ...

The Lights change for Scene 2

SCENE 2

In front of the warehouse. That night

In the darkness, the shadowy silhouettes of Richard and Nathan come into view. A can of gasoline is at their side. The burning warehouse glows in front of them

Richard It needs more gasoline.
Nathan I'm scared.
Richard More gasoline, Nathan.

Nathan doesn't budge. Richard hands him the gas can and orders him

Now!

Nathan relents and throws a splash of gasoline off into the distance. This causes immense flames to illuminate Nathan and Richard fully

Nathan (*panicked*) OK. Now let's get out of here.
Richard Get out of here? You chicken-shit! We have to stay and watch.
Nathan But ... what if the warehouse ...
Richard Relax, Nathan. (*He pulls Nathan down on to the ground with him*)

Richard practically sun-bathes in the glow of the fire as the music begins

Isn't it beautiful?
Nathan It's something.

Richard places an arm around Nathan, pulling him in close

This reminds me of high school.
Richard Yeah. The night I torched the records office.

Richard continues to relax in the warmth

Look at it smoulder! It's breathtaking! And you know what a little misdemeanour does for me, Babe.
Nathan You haven't called me "Babe" in a long time.
Richard (*playfully*) Because I know you like it.
Nathan That is cruel, you son of a bitch.
Richard You like that too. I guess the name still fits. You're still awfully tiny.
Nathan You'd be surprised how I've grown. (*He faces Richard squarely and makes a demand*) Touch me.
Richard Ask me nicer.
Nathan Fuck you!
Richard Fuck you back!
Nathan Please touch me.

Richard softly caresses Nathan as he begins to sing, keeping one eye on the fire

No. 5 Nothing Like A Fire

Richard   There's nothing like
                   A warm, romantic fire
                   To put me in the proper frame of mind.
                   There's nothing like a roaring, raging fire
                   To help me unwind.

He begins to massage Nathan's shoulders

                   There's nothing like
                   The sound of crackling embers
                   To calm me when my pulse begins to race
                   There's nothing like the glow of sizzling embers
                   To brighten your face.

Music continues

Nathan (*speaking*) Shouldn't we take this someplace else? The fire brigade could be here any minute.

Richard (*speaking*) You're the look-out. Tell me if you see anything big and red coming.

Nathan giggles and cuddles closer to Richard

    (*Singing*)   Feel the heat intensify
                       Watch the sparks begin to fly
                       Watch the smoke fill up the sky —
                       Straight to the stars!

Nathan (*singing*) — Straight to the stars!

Richard   There's nothing like
                       The sight of something burning —

Nathan   Something burning …

Richard   — to soothe me
                       With a hot seductive light —

Nathan   Seductive light …

Richard   There's nothing like
                       The smell of something burning —

Nathan   Something burning …

Richard   — to start to ignite
                       My desire …

Both   There's nothing like a fire!
                       Feel the heat intensify,
                       Watch the sparks begin to fly
                       Watch the smoke fill up the sky —
                       Clouding the night!
                       There's nothing like a fire!

Richard and Nathan proceed to get intimate. The glow of the fire grows bigger, brighter and hotter and finally fades

The Lights quickly shift back to the distinct parole board room look

Nathan I didn't see him at all the next day. It was torture. Finally I couldn't take it any longer and I showed up at his house real late that night …

The Lights change for Scene 3

SCENE 3

Richard's bedroom. The next night

Richard is resting and reclining, engrossed in his Nietzsche book. He looks up and sees Nathan standing in front of him

Richard (*startled*) Who the hell let you in?
Nathan Your brother.
Richard John? I'll strangle him.
Nathan I thought I'd surprise you.
Richard Why?
Nathan So I could thank you for last night.
Richard You're welcome. Goodbye. (*He turns his attention back to the book*)
Nathan What are you reading?
Richard Nietzsche. But I'm finished. (*He puts the book down, and tries to give Nathan the brush off*) And now "superior man" must go to sleep.
Nathan Great!
Richard Alone.
Nathan I told my dad I wasn't coming home tonight.
Richard Why did you do that?
Nathan I thought I could stay over.
Richard Who invited you? I didn't.
Nathan I'll get John to invite me then.
Richard Fine. Stay. You're welcome to watch me sleep.
Nathan Thank you. (*He makes himself comfortable*)

Music begins

Can we talk for a while?
Richard No.
Nathan I'm worried.
Richard Now what?

No. 6 A Written Contract ("Superior", Part 1)

Nathan (*singing*) How could I ever face my dad
                              If he found out we burned that
                              Warehouse down?

Richard (*singing*) It was the best evening
             That we ever had!
             And no one will ever know.

Nathan   Can you be sure?

The music continues

Richard It's right here, Nathan, in black and white. And Nietzsche
doesn't lie! (*He hands Nathan the book and points to a passage. He
sings*)
             We're superior
             We are supermen
             Says my Nietzsche book
             Chapters one thru' ten
             And as supermen
             We could not get caught.
             So don't give last night a second thought.
             Let's plan next time —

             'Cause we're both superior, I quote:
             "The superman is above all of society"
             We'll have Chicago by the throat,
             If you help me —
             Remember you're my look-out, Babe!

The music continues. Nathan feigns thumbing through the book

Nathan In which chapter does Nietzsche talk about arson? I bet that's
a good one! You *know* if we pull any more of this stupid stuff we can
kiss law school goodbye.
Richard With *me* in charge? We're a productive team. And we should
do a lot more than just burn down old warehouses ...
Nathan I don't want to do any of it. (*He moves to touch Richard*) Can't
we just ...
Richard (*moving away*) If you don't want to be part of my fun, I'm
certainly not going to be part of yours. You know that by now.
Nathan I thought our relationship had matured.
Richard You were wrong. And you might as well go home now, Nathan.
Have a swell summer. And a nice life.
Nathan I'm not trying to stop *you*, but you don't need my help breaking
the law.
Richard (*reluctantly*) Yes I do ... I ... I screw up without you.
Nathan What?

Richard I screw up without you, OK!
Nathan You never said you needed me before.

Richard stays silent as Nathan contemplates

I can't do this, Richard. You'll double cross me. I'll do what you want,
but you won't do what I want.
Richard I'm really disappointed in you, Nathan. You were making such
progress, but now ...

The music intensifies. Richard sings

No. 7 A Written Contract (Part 2)

You're not fit to
Pour me bath-tub booze
You don't deserve me!
You're not fit to
Lick my wing-tip shoes!
You just unnerve me!
Since I haven't learned when
No means no, Babe.
I'm gonna tempt your brain
With quid-pro-quo, Babe!
A written contract!

Nathan (*speaking*) A written contract?

Richard   Spelling out what you will do for me:
Participation
In my crimes, no matter what degree!
For compensation, I'll agree
To any terms you lay out!
So that means when you ask
I'll have no way out.
A written contract!
Here's your chance
To make things legal at last
In plain black and white
We can let the past remain in the past
And have no more reason to fight!

Richard gets a portable Underwood typewriter out from a hiding place

> I'll even let you
> Type the whole thing out —
> Each key provision!

Richard sets the typewriter down. It glistens in the light

> Wipe away that look of fear and doubt,
> Make a decision!
> Don't hold out, you'll get
> No better offer!
> 'Cause it's the only option I can proffer!
> A formal contract,
> A written contract
> Will help to get you yours
> And I'll get mine!
> But you'll never be my equal
> If you don't promise me you'll sign!

The music continues. Richard sits Nathan in front of the typewriter

Nathan (*speaking*) Isn't this the typewriter you swiped from your roommate freshman year?
Richard Be careful. That's a very valuable Underwood.

Nathan types a few strokes

Nathan It's also busted. The "c" is dropped. And the "t" is really faint.
Richard Shut up and take this down …
Nathan One second, I need my glasses.

Nathan pulls a pair of reading glasses out of a pocket and puts them on. Then he types as Richard dictates

No. 8 A Written Contract (Part 3)

Richard   "I, Nathan Leopold
> Hereby swear to aid and abet
> At Richard's request.
> No matter what he wants
> I'll give him my best ——

Nathan   — But only as much as I get!"

Richard (*speaking*) Whatever.

Nathan (*happily*) Now it's my turn. (*He sings as he types*)

> "In consideration of
> The above,
> I, Richard Loeb
> Swear to *satisfy* Babe —
> Wherever it leads
> Immediately following the above.
> I'll give him whatever he needs!"

The music continues

Richard Fine, now finish it off with a couple of whereases and wherefores …
Nathan This is great practice for contract law class.
Richard Type.

Nathan types a few closing words and pulls the contract out of the carriage

Nathan Done.
Richard Great. Now comes the good part.

Richard pulls a sharp-looking pocket-knife out of his pocket

Nathan Why a knife?
Richard We have to sign in blood.
Nathan What are you, a fucking Indian? Why?
Richard Because I said so. And because it's more binding that way. Trust me, you'll enjoy a little pain. Hold out your finger.

Nathan doesn't

Hold out your finger!

Richard forcefully grabs Nathan's hand then gently sings

No. 9 A Written Contract (Part 4)

> All I have to do is
> Take the knife
> And gently puncture the skin.

Richard attempts to stab, but Nathan pulls away. Richard grabs his finger again

I've done this before! (*He succeeds*)

Nathan Ouch! Shit!
Richard Sign your name.

Nathan signs in blood

(*Singing*)   And once the blood has dried,
                 The terms will begin!

Nathan shakes his finger. Richard grabs it

Try not to drip on the floor!

Nathan (*speaking*) Do I get to do you now?
Richard No, I can take care of myself.

Richard plunges the blade into his own finger, causing Nathan to wince. He carefully signs his name. Nathan grasps Richard's hand to seal the pact

Nathan (*singing*) Now our lives will be —

Both   Entwined completely!
                   Our friendship's now redefined,
                   Rethought and revised!

Nathan   No turning back now
                   Since our blood's been combined!

Richard drops Nathan's hand and gives him the contract

Richard   But not 'til it's been notarized!

Nathan folds it and puts it in his pocket. While keeping a close eye on each other, they sing

Both   And no one has to know
                   Our business deal
                   We'll keep it hidden!
                   All attempts to break our private seal
                   Will be forbidden.
                   It's the same old game

> With one new feature.
> And next semester
> You can show your teacher
> A simple contract,
> A written contract
> The clauses not misleading,
> The print not fine!
> And I hope the contract is the answer
> To finally keeping you in line!

Nathan removes his glasses. Richard snaps his knife shut

The Lights change to reflect the parole board

Nathan We kept things simple at first. Just silly crimes really ... nothing that would hurt anyone. For a while he kept his end of the bargain and it was great. But after a few weeks I noticed a change ...

The Lights change for Scene 4

SCENE 4

Nathan's bedroom. A few weeks later

Nathan and Richard race breathlessly into the room. Nathan carries a bag full of stolen loot

Richard Not bad, Babe! You were quicker with the signal this time!
Nathan (*catching his breath*) Thank God. Another five seconds and we would have been caught red-handed!
Richard But we weren't.
Nathan We've never had that close a call. I knew we shouldn't risk breaking into someone's house while they were asleep. Stores are so much easier.
Richard It was thrilling for *me*.
Nathan How can you be so damned calm?
Richard Because worrying is *your* department. Give me the bag, let's look at all this junk.

Nathan hands him the bag. Richard opens it. Nathan loosens his tie and starts to get comfortable

Music begins

Richard pulls a few things out of the bag, such as a silver tray, candlesticks, etc. Nathan tries to get his attention by running his fingers through Richard's hair. Richard brushes him away

Richard Quit it.
Nathan (*irritated*) It's my turn.

Richard rummages through the bag, with growing disappointment as Nathan becomes increasingly annoyed

Richard This is all shit. I'm throwing everything away. If you want something, claim it now.
Nathan I want *you*. Hold me.

Richard, having paid no attention, snaps his fingers, getting an idea

Richard How about we rob my father's office tomorrow night? That would *really* be a thrill … there's this back door that no one knows about, with a really crummy lock. Easy to pick. And he's got a bunch of gold coins and a big stamp collection in his safe … I think the combination is John's birthday …

No longer able to contain his feelings, Nathan sings

No. 10 Thrill Me

Nathan (*angrily*) Don't bore me with details
They'll never impress me
Start paying attention
Don't try to finesse me!
Thrill me … thrill me!

Richard (*speaking*) Thrill yourself.

Nathan   Don't forget what you promised
On paper —
What you'd do when we finished a caper!
Every time I demand what's required
You complain that you're simply too tired.
Thrill me!

Richard starts to close up the bag carefully. Nathan pushes it away

>   Don't toy with distractions.
>   Why fuel my frustration?
>   You're trying to cheat me!
>   What's your explanation?
>   Thrill me ... thrill me!

Richard (*speaking*) I don't feel like it. I feel kinda down lately. It's not exciting any more. Break the window, pick the lock, steal things we don't need. It's all too easy ... there's no "thrill" left.

Nathan (*singing*) If this keeps going on
>   I'll go crazy!
>   I'm aroused, you're conveniently lazy!
>   So my rage and impatience keep growing
>   But they get my adrenaline going!
>   Thrill me!

>   Don't think up excuses
>   They'll never persuade me
>   Let's turn all the lights off
>   Don't try to evade me!
>   Thrill me!

Nathan tries to unfasten Richard's trousers

Richard (*speaking*) Stop that!

(*Singing*)   Until I feel energized
>   I will not be in the mood!

Nathan   I've held back
>   And I've compromised
>   So, unless you want to get sued ...

>   Why spoil my evening?
>   And why must you deny me?
>   I'll stop my complaining
>   Once you satisfy me!
>   Won't you thrill me?

Music continues to pulse

Richard I said *no*.
Nathan Will you ever be square with me?
Richard Sure. Just not now.
Nathan I'm sick of hearing that! The only reason I've been helping
you do these stupid things is because we have a contract ... (*He grabs
the contract from its hiding place and waves it in Richard's face*) ...
signed in blood! You want me to tear it up?
Richard No. OK, OK. You win. Let's make it fast though. I've gotta get
up early. (*He starts to take off his tie and untuck his shirt*)
Nathan Don't be unfocused, Richard —

Nathan sings while unbuttoning his shirt, as Richard throws off his own

> But don't treat me with kid gloves
> I'll always obey you!
> One perfect accomplice,
> Who'd never betray you
> If you thrill me!
> Thrill me! (*He reaches for Richard*)

The Lights change for Scene 5

SCENE 5

Parole board hearing room at Joliet Prison. 1958

Nathan once again faces the unseen parole board

Parole Board Voice 1 Mr Leopold, you went along with him every
time. What did you think would happen if you didn't?
Nathan He'd never see me again. I never really believed that we'd
go as far as he wanted. His friendship was necessary to me. I had no
choice.
Parole Board Voice 2 (*sceptically*) Friendship?
Nathan (*quietly*) We were very close. The point is I would do whatever
he asked.
Parole Board Voice 1 You were not in control of your own actions?
That's hard to believe, Mr Leopold.
Nathan I don't know how my conscience worked then.
Parole Board Voice 2 How exactly did Loeb convince you to commit
the crime?

Nathan It was a little later that same night … about five minutes later …

The Lights change for Scene 6. Nathan takes his place with Richard

SCENE 6

Nathan's bedroom. A few minutes after Scene 4

Nathan, smiling and pleased with himself, begins to re-tie his tie and button his clothes back up. Richard slips his shirt back on and lights a cigarette

Richard You know what would thrill *me*, Nathan?
Nathan What?
Richard A more important crime. A *superior* crime. Burglary and setting fires are too trivial for supermen like us.
Nathan What do you think would be more appropriate?
Richard Something we could be proud of.
Nathan *Armed* robbery? (*He giggles*)
Richard Murder.

Shocked, Nathan searches for a response

Nathan You've been reading too much Nietzsche. And way too many detective magazines.
Richard I'm serious.
Nathan Murder is a big leap, even for you.
Richard No, no, no. It's a *logical progression*.
Nathan Forget it.
Richard Scared?

Nathan doesn't respond

As of tonight we're even. Now you have to help me or you'll break the contract.
Nathan This is crazy. What would possess you to want to kill somebody?
Richard The challenge, fool. Think of how incredibly significant it would be.
Nathan *Now* you're scaring me.
Richard But that's what you like, isn't it?
Nathan Not if it involves the death penalty.

Richard (*cavalierly*) Forget the death penalty. We're not amateur idiots. We're smart. We're going to be lawyers!

Nathan But it's wrong.

Richard Says who?

Nathan Says anyone. Society.

Richard (*passionately*) We are above society. Murder is the only crime worthy of our talents, Nathan. Don't you want to do something important with your life?

Nathan (*exasperated*) I don't believe you're serious. It's the stupidest … craziest … who would you want to … kill?

Richard You know.

Nathan No. I have no idea.

Richard Who irks me the most?

Nathan Me?

Richard Besides you.

Music creeps in

Nathan Who the hell are you talking about?

Richard sings

No. 11 The Plan

Richard
If we killed my brother John
Then he'd never touch my things!
If we killed my brother John
Then he'd never rat me out
If we killed my brother John
My inheritance would grow ——

Nathan tries to treat it all as a joke

Nathan
You're a lunatic! Come on!
Can't we let the subject go?

Richard
We could chloroform a rag
And make him breathe the vapours
Then use it as a gag
To choke him.
And once his face is green
We'll throw him in a bag
Flee the murder scene
Then read about it in the papers.

                        If we killed my brother John
                        Then my father would drop dead!
                        If we killed my brother John
                        Then I'd get the bigger room.
                        If we killed my brother John
                        Like I've always yearned to do ——

Nathan   If you killed your brother John,
                        Every lead would point to *you!*

*Richard pays no attention to Nathan, who grows more and more
uncomfortable*

Richard   We could borrow some old gun
                        And shoot him in his slumber
                        Perhaps it would be fun
                        To torture him!
                        We'll make it look like rape!
                        And once the deed is done
                        We'll misdirect the cops
                        And watch his name
                        Become a number!

                        If we killed my brother John ——

Nathan   You could never practise law.
Richard   If we killed my brother John ——
Nathan   You could never face your mother!
Both   If we killed my/your brother John ——
Nathan   Could you live with what you did?

A pause. Richard thinks for a moment

Richard   OK, not my brother John.
                        Let's go kill some *random* kid!

The music continues

Nathan (*sarcastically*) Oh, that's much better. Much better.
Richard It's perfect. All we have to do is go down to our old elementary
    school, after the last bell …
Nathan Wouldn't kidnapping be enough?
Richard Brilliant! This man is a fucking genius! We'll do *both!*
Nathan Both?!

Richard We'll kill him, but first find out his name and address then gouge his folks for a ransom. I could write a note. They'll think he's still alive.

Nathan What happens if they find the body?

Richard (*oblivious*) This is perfect. I bet we could get five or ten thousand.

Nathan We don't need money.

Richard You don't. But my father's been awfully stingy lately. Come on, Babe ... (*He caresses Nathan gently*) You know how excited it'll make me. Let's see ... a ten or eleven-year-old ...

Richard sings into Nathan's ear, stroking his hair, holding his hand ... drawing him in

> I'll lure him to my car
> Then strike with something sizeable.
> We'll drive out extra far
> To dump him.
> Pour acid on his face
> And every birthmark, mole or scar.
> Then strip off all his clothing
> So he'll be unrecognizable!

Both
Richard
> Just a boy who's in the park—
> Won't be smart enough to run.

Both
Richard
> Just a kid who's in the dark —
> Won't be strong enough to fight!

Both
Richard
> Bait the fish to feed the shark —
> Thirty seconds and he's gone.

Nathan
> What a way to make your mark!

Richard gets right into Nathan's face

Richard
> Better than my brother John!

The Lights change. Nathan addresses the parole board

Nathan Richard needed three days to get ready.

The Lights change for Scene 7

SCENE 7

Richard's garage, a few weeks later/the parole board room. 1958

The music changes. Richard kneels on the ground with the murder weapons — a rope, a crowbar and a small bottle of acid — in front of him with a leather case. He talks as if to Nathan. However, Nathan is still presented in front of the parole board on the opposite side of the stage

The Lights continually shift back and forth between the two spaces and the two different time periods

Richard Rope, crowbar, acid. That's everything.

Richard inspects the weapons as Nathan stands before the parole board

I hope this rope is strong enough. It's *not* the kind I told you to get.

The Lights shift to Nathan's space. Nathan sings to the parole board

No. 12 Way Too Far

Nathan It had gone way too far
Yet there I was assisting
It had gone way too far
I was acting like his prisoner
Much too late to start resisting.

The Lights shift to Richard's space

Richard (*speaking*) The crowbar, however, is per-fect-o.

The Lights shift to Nathan's space

Nathan How did it come to this?
Was something wrong inside me?
How did it come to this?
It was impossible to run away
Or let my conscience guide me.

The Lights shift to Richard's space

Richard This is a damned small bottle of acid. I guess we'll have to find a damned small boy.

Richard packs the weapons into the leather case. The Lights shift to Nathan's space. Nathan continues to sing

Nathan   He thought it was fun.
                    His dark side
                    Was difficult to swallow.
                    Not difficult to follow
                    I tried to stay calm
                    I tried to stay sane.
                    The heart is a muscle
                    That I can't explain!

                    What made me feel this way?
                    And made him so exciting?
                    What made me feel this way?
                    Should have somehow tried to make it stop
                    But had no use in fighting.

The music continues. The Lights shift to Richard's space

Richard I'm putting *you* in charge of writing down his address for the ransom note. So, when I've got the rope around his neck, you say "if you wanna live, give me your address." Then once you have it, I'll crack his skull. (*He grabs the leather case*) I'll meet you at the car.

Richard exits

The Lights shift to Nathan's space

Nathan   It soon would be done
                    And then he'd be tied to me forever
                    I'm smart, but he was clever.
                    Too late to say no ...
                    I walked to his car ...
                    Forced myself to be much stronger
                    If for just a little longer!
                    Then I let it go too far.

The Lights change for Scene 8

SCENE 8

Near the school yard. A few hours later

Richard enters, illuminated only by the glowing headlights of his car which cast his looming shadow across the yard

Through billows of exhaust, Nathan can barely be seen watching, horrified, but remaining a loyal lookout

Finally, Richard spots a target. His eyes follow an (unseen) young boy on the other side of the yard. He first gets his attention with a wave and then sings to him

No. 13 Roadster

Richard   Would you like to see my roadster?
Would you like to look inside?
It's a shiny Packard roadster.
Would you like to take a ride?
A spin around the block?
I'd be glad to drop you off!

Richard holds out his cigarette case in an attempt to lure the boy, but to no avail. He continues

We could cruise around the school yard,
Be the envy of your pals.
If you're riding with me shotgun,
You'll impress the pretty gals.

See it sitting in the alley?
Couldn't find a parking space.
We could open up the windows,
Wind will whip across your face!
Go climb inside the car.
I'd be glad to drop you off.

As if stopping the boy from walking away, Richard quickly tries a different tactic

I know — never talk to strangers!
That's what mothers always warn.

But I think we could be buddies.
Sure, I'll let you honk the horn.
I think you need a lift.
I'd be glad to drop you off.

Feel the power of my engine
When it speeds to forty five —

He reaches into his pocket and pulls out the ignition-lock key, holding it up almost hypnotically

Here's the key to the ignition.
Take the wheel, I'll let you drive!
Or hop inside the back.
I'll be glad to drop you off.

The boy has clearly taken the bait

Just tell me where you live.
I'll be glad to drop you off.

(*Speaking*) What's your name? (*He crooks his head to listen*) Bobby's a nice name … (*He beckons the boy to follow and walks off*)

(*Singing*)   You'll be safe inside my roadster!

Richard exits. After a moment, Nathan follows

Lights fade to near black, then change for Scene 9

SCENE 9

The woods near Wolf Lake. Later that night (after the murder)

The music pulses

Richard and Nathan rush in. Richard carries a blood-stained rag along with the used murder weapons. He is breathless but truly exhilarated. Nathan holds a bloody rag and the empty leather case. He looks off in horror toward the site of the murder and frantically sings

No. 14 Superior

Nathan   All of Chicago would go mad
                  If they discovered what we did tonight.

Richard draws his attention

Richard (*singing*) But we're both superior, be glad!
                  How could they ever catch two geniuses?

                  Twenty feet from here
                  In a culvert pipe
                  Lies a twelve-year-old
                  Whose time was ripe!
                  Just a useless kid ... (*He waves the empty acid bottle*)
                  With no face, and thus
                  They could never tie a thing to us!

Richard hands the bottle to a frozen Nathan

                  No evidence!
                  And that's why —

Both   We're both superior to all,
                  We've got more intelligence than anyone!

Richard   We roll Chicago like a ball

Richard snaps the murder rope loudly, making Nathan jump

                  And we're far more efficient
                  Than the mob is, Babe!

Nathan   I'm overcome ...
                  I'm feeling numb!

Richard hands Nathan the crowbar

Richard   Wipe the crowbar clean! (*He throws him the rope*)
                  Don't forget the rope! (*He throws him the bloody rag*)
                  Wash the blood stains off
                  With kitchen soap!

Nathan quickly places all the weapons into the bag

> Then destroy it all
> And don't leave a trace!

Nathan   I'm afraid they'll see it
                    On my face!

Richard   You're paranoid!
                    Just tell yourself:

Both   We're both superior to all!
                    We simply function on a higher plane!

Richard   We'll let Chicago take the fall!
                    There's no shortage of perverts
                    They can blame it on!

Nathan   But I told myself
                    That this was all a game
                    I'm still in shock,
                    Why don't you feel the same?

Richard   How many times must I address your doubts?
                    We've vandalized,
                    Burglarized
                    And never left a clue
                    This was no risk —
                    And fun to do!

Richard moves toward Nathan

> So, let me ease your mind,
> Try to understand,
> And enjoy the fact
> It went as planned.

Nathan tries to back away

Nathan   You're scaring me!

Richard grabs Nathan

Richard   Then don't forget —

Both   We're both superior to all!
                            We've got a bond,
                            We'll take it to the grave!

Richard   We've backed Chicago to the wall!

Nathan   And you're sure that we weren't seen?
Richard (*speaking*) Yes!

Nathan   There's no chance we'll be accused —
Richard No!

Nathan   You guarantee our hands are clean?
Richard Yes!

Nathan   Tell me what's next, I'm all confused!

Richard (*singing*) We'll write the ransom note, all right?
Nathan (*speaking*) All right!

Richard   When we're at home and out of sight!
Nathan All right!

Richard   Make sure you duck if you see light —
Nathan All right!

Richard   Now let's cap off one superior ...

Richard beckons Nathan towards him

                            ... night! (*He pulls Nathan in for a tight embrace*)

Nathan (*singing*) This has gone way too far!

The Lights change. Nathan solemnly addresses the parole board

  (*Speaking*) I had never seen him so happy. We went back to his house
  ... I was shaking the whole way ... he got out the Underwood ...

The Lights change for Scene 10

Scene 10

Richard's bedroom. Later that night

Richard sits at his typewriter, typing the last few strokes of the ransom note. Nathan nervously paces

Music pulses

Richard How do you spell "valise"?
Nathan V-A-L-I-S-E.

Richard types the last word and with a flourish, pulls the paper off the carriage

Richard Not bad. Read it with me, Babe.

Nathan fishes in his pocket

Nathan That's strange.
Richard What?
Nathan My glasses?
Richard Your glasses what?
Nathan I can't imagine where I ...
Richard Come on, just squint!

Nathan goes to him. Richard puts his arm around Nathan, and holds the document up for him

Music begins

No. 15 Ransom Note

They sing slowly in unison

Both   If you want to see your son,
                           Then you'll follow every rule
                           He is safely here unharmed
                           And, so far, we've not been cruel.
                           Get ten thousand in small bills
                           And make sure there's no police
                           Then drive straight to Jackson Park
                           And wait there for his release!

Richard	If you want to see your son …
Nathan	If you want to see your son …
Richard	Make the nightmare quickly cease —
Nathan	Make the nightmare quickly cease!
Richard	Leave the cash in Jackson Park
Nathan	Leave the cash in Jackson Park —
Richard	In a brand-new black valise!
Nathan	In a brand-new black valise!

The music continues

Richard (*speaking*) Perfect so far.
Nathan (*speaking*) Perfect so far.

Richard rolls the paper back into the typewriter

Richard I wonder what my father would do if I was kidnapped.
Nathan He'd pay.
Richard Maybe he'd pay.
Nathan Of course he'd pay. He's loaded.
Richard Maybe.
Nathan I know my dad would pay to get me back.
Richard Of course. You're his precious little Nathan. My father and I don't have that kind of relationship. He'd only be worried about bad publicity for him.
Nathan (*caringly*) He wouldn't let you die.
Richard Well, let's hope I never have to find out. (*He continues to type the final lines as they sing*)

Both	If you want to see your son …
	Be alone when you arrive.
Richard	Do exactly as we say —
Both	Then you'll get him back alive…
	Yes, you'll get him back alive…

Richard removes the note from the typewriter and hands it to Nathan to deliver

Yes, you'll get him back alive …

Nathan takes the note from Richard

Lights change for Scene 11

SCENE 11

Nathan's house and Richard's house. The days following the murder

The sound of static then a radio broadcast is heard in virtual darkness

Radio Newscaster voice … reached a record one hundred and two degrees in Cicero. In local news, last night the disfigured body of what is believed to be a young boy was discovered half-dangling from a culvert pipe at Wolf Lake. Police warn the public to stay out of the woods near that area after dark. In sports, Chicago's Cubbies once again were beaten by the New York …

The radio fades out and an isolated light comes up on Nathan with a candlestick-style telephone

Music pulses

Nathan (*into the phone*) Hello, John? May I please speak to your brother? Tell him it's important. Very important.

Another isolated light comes up on Richard, also with a candlestick-style telephone

Richard Hello, Nathan.
Nathan Richard, have you seen the *Tribune*?
Richard Yes.

No. 16 My Glasses/Just Lay Low

Nathan (*singing*) How could they have found the boy? I'm shaking!
I thought you said we had the perfect spot!
Could I have dropped my glasses there?
Why can't I find them anywhere?
They were inside my pocket, now they're not!

Richard (*speaking*) So they found the body. That's *all* they have. They can't even be sure who it is! His face is gone.

(*Singing*)	We'll lay low a few days longer And you'll see, they have no case This will all die down eventually, There's nothing they can trace!
Nathan	If we wait a few days longer And get caught — then there's no hope! But if we turn ourselves in now ...
Richard	They'll stick our necks inside a rope! Don't even suggest that, They have no leads So we're still fine!
Nathan	But, my glasses ...
Richard	Forget your goddamned glasses, And get off the goddamned line!

They both hang up. The Lights change to reflect the passage of time. The music continues

Another radio broadcast is heard

Radio Newscaster voice ... following up on yesterday's gruesome discovery, the mutilated boy has been identified as Bobby Franks, son of the wealthy Chicago family ...

Nathan, on the phone, speaks to Richard again

Nathan They know it's Bobby Franks!!! They identified a birthmark on his back. Why didn't you turn him over?
Richard I forgot, OK?! (*He sings*)

	I can't believe we lost ten thousand dollars The ransom scheme's a bust, the plans are dead! Don't show up at the drop tonight — I'm sure that they'll stake out the site!
Nathan	I knew it wouldn't work, The way you said! And I'm convinced I must have dropped My glasses. I know I had them on inside your car ...

| Richard | I planned this all out perfectly, |
| | I need you to stay calm for me — |

| Nathan | — I wish I could remember |
| | Where they are! |

Richard	Just lay low a few days longer
	And you'll see they'll have no clues
	There is no need to be nervous
	There's no way we're gonna lose
	Just listen to me, Babe!
	You're not alone!

| Nathan | But my glasses ... |

| Richard | Oh, screw your goddamned glasses! |
| | And get off the goddamned phone! |

They both hang up. The Lights change to reflect the passage of time again. Music continues

Another broadcast

Radio Newscaster voice ... And the Chicago police believe that the pair of eye-glasses found near the scene may provide answers in the shocking murder of Bobby Franks. In other news ...

Nathan is discovered in a true panic

Nathan	The *Herald* says they found a pair of glasses
	I think that it's a very scary sign!
	They gave it seven paragraphs
	And printed lots of photographs
	The glasses look an awful lot like *mine*!

The music stops dead. Richard practically drops the phone. Then he calmly and slowly sings to Nathan

| Richard | But they're just a pair of glasses |
| | Not the murder weapon! |

Nathan	True.
	But it means they found a link to us ...
Richard	Not to "us", Babe, but to *you*!

Nathan (*horrified; speaking*) Richard!

Music continues in full tempo

Richard   Just lay low a few days longer
And the news will fade away
We just have to play it safe
No matter what the papers say!

Nathan	**Richard**
I'm convinced I must have	Just lay low a few days
Dropped my glasses	Longer and their case will
There must be thousands	Lose its steam
Out there just like mine	There's no choice you
But I had them on	Must be stronger
Inside your car and	Have to take one for the team!
Now I don't know	Just lay low
Where they are!	Just lay low, just lay low
It sends an icy chill	Just lay low, just lay low
Right down my spine!	Just lay low, just lay low!

Richard listens as Nathan tries not to go to pieces. Nathan sings

Nathan   There may have been a witness near the lake ...

Richard (*speaking*) No ...

Nathan   We might have left a footprint in the mud ...

Richard We didn't ...

Nathan   Suppose we weren't too careful with the blood ...

Richard We were careful ...

Nathan   Or maybe made some other huge mistake!

They put the phones down and sing their internal thoughts

Nathan	**Richard**
It's all starting to unravel.	Just lay low a few days longer
The next sound we hear	And their case will turn to crap
Will be the gavel!	There's no choice. You must be
	Stronger, don't you fall inside
	Their trap!

They bring the phones back to their ears and sing to each other

Both   Can't you understand this situation?

Nathan   I think *I* understand and clearly see!
                      They found my glasses
                      And it won't take long
                      Before they find me!

Richard   Just lay low!
Nathan   We need a plan "B"
Richard   Just lay low!
Nathan   Just lay low?
Both   Just lay low!

They both hang up forcefully

The Lights change to illuminate the parole board room as Nathan takes his place

SCENE 12

The parole board hearing room. 1958

Nathan stands in front of the parole board. Music punctuates the scene

Parole Board Voice 1 All of the books that have been written about you go into considerable detail about the crime. But there's not a lot about your police interrogations. Not even in your book.
Nathan It didn't seem important.
Parole Board Voice 2 Not important? I suppose it's true that the Chicago police in nineteen twenty-four were not what you would call the world's most thorough law enforcement agency.
Parole Board Voice 1 Of course, they hadn't had much experience talking over sordid details like those.
Parole Board Voice 2 With homicidal degenerates ——
Nathan (*interrupting*) That's not how I would characterize it.
Parole Board Voice 1 Tell us about the police investigation ... how you were caught ...
Nathan After they found the glasses, the police wanted to see me. It was shocking how fast they found me ...

The Lights change for Scene 13

SCENE 13

Nathan's bedroom. A few days later

Nathan nervously waits. Finally Richard calmly enters the room

Richard I got here as soon as I could. Tell me exactly what the cops said.

Nathan (*frantically*) It was all about the frame hinges being rare. How only three people in the state have them. My show-off dad wanted me to have the latest thing. The cops traced them through my optometrist.

Richard See what having "the best" gets you? And you said what?

Nathan I said "oh". Then they asked if I had lost them. And I said yes.

Richard You said yes?

Nathan I had to.

Richard And ...

Nathan And they're gonna pick me up tomorrow morning to identify them. If it wasn't for my dad's reputation they wouldn't be so accommodating. They must've wanted me to have time to get a lawyer.

Richard (*coolly*) You've got a lawyer — you've got *me*. I'll tell you what to say.

Nathan What can I say? They've got my glasses ...

Richard The fact that they were there doesn't prove they have anything to do with the kid. You'll explain you were with your bird-watching class last Sunday and you must have dropped them then. It's a perfectly reasonable explanation.

Nathan What if they want to know where I was Wednesday night? My dad knows I wasn't home.

Richard Nobody can be expected to rattle off exactly what they were doing on an ordinary weeknight. So don't offer the cops too much or it'll sound fake. Just pretend to keep trying to think. Remember, cops are dumber than dirt! And whatever you do, don't you mention me.

Nathan I'm scared shitless, Richard.

Music begins. Richard sits Nathan down

Richard You're gonna be fine. I'll tell you precisely what to say when they stare you down with their big pasty faces ...

No. 17 I'm Trying To Think

Richard sings while coaching Nathan

Richard	Yes I remember the night—
Nathan	— The night.
Richard	Last Wednesday I went for a drive.
Nathan	—For a drive!
Richard	I stopped for a cheap little bite—
Nathan	— For a bite.
Richard	And picked up some girl in some dive
Nathan	— And picked up some *girl* in some dive!?!!!
Richard	I'm trying to think!
Nathan	I'm trying to think!
Richard	They'll want the details.
Nathan	You want the details?
Richard	She wore something pink —
Nathan	She wore something pink,
	And had painted nails!

Richard (*speaking*) That's good!

(*Singing*)	You're trying to think ...
Nathan	Trying to think!
Richard	Trying to think!
Both	Trying to think!

Nathan (*speaking*) They'll wanna know about the girl.
Richard OK ... OK ... Let me think ...

(*Singing*)	No, I don't remember her face—
Nathan	— I don't remember her face!
Richard	And she never told me her name!
Nathan	— She never told me her name.
Richard	I wish I could help with this case
Nathan	— I wish I could help with this case!

Both   But all of those girls are the same!

Nathan   I'm trying to think!
Richard   Keep trying to think!
                    And don't act like you're holding something back.
                    You don't have anything to hide,
                    You're not gonna crack!

(*Speaking*) Now, the most important part, the cop'll probably say —

(*Singing*)   Were you *alone* with the girl?
Nathan   — We were alone, she and I

Richard   You're not one to lie or pretend?
Nathan   — I'm not one to lie or pretend!

Richard   So is she your sole alibi?
Nathan   — I guess she's my sole alibi!

Both   The wrong type on which to depend!
                    But a girl there's no need to defend!

Richard   Keep trying to think!

Nathan starts to lose his concentration. Richard tries to remain patient

Nathan   I remember … the night?
Richard   Keep trying to think!
Nathan   Don't remember … her name?
Richard   Keep trying to think!
Nathan   No, we were … alone?
Both   Keep trying to think!
Nathan   Keep trying to think …

Music continues

(*Speaking*) Are you sure that I can do this?
Richard Yes. Remember Nietzsche. You're superior to them all.

Richard starts to leave. Nathan attempts to stop him

Nathan I wish you could be there with me.

Richard tries to be as tender to him as possible

Richard I can't be connected to it. You'll be OK, Babe. You'll convince
them. And meet me at Jackson Park when you're through.

Richard exits

*Nathan nervously sings as a lighting transition suggests he is being
questioned by the police under a harsh interrogation light*

Nathan   I remember the night!
                   Don't remember her name!
                   No, we were alone!
                   I'm trying to think …
                   I'm trying to think!

The Lights change. Nathan speaks to the parole board

The next morning at the police station was the most … I'd never gone
through anything like it before … But I got through it and I needed to
be with Richard more than ever …

The Lights change for Scene 14

SCENE 14

Jackson Park. The next afternoon

*Nathan, who is now much more relaxed, waits in the park. Richard
arrives, barely hiding his nervousness. He approaches Nathan*

Richard How did it go?
Nathan I had to come up with a version of the whole thing to tell my
dad first. He wanted to know everything.
Richard Did anyone follow you here?
Nathan I don't think so.
Richard Tell me about the police.
Nathan I did exactly what you said. You were right. They believed me.
Richard Or they just wanted you to think they did.
Nathan That's crazy. They let me go.
Richard You didn't mention my name at all, did you?
Nathan It never came up. I told them I dropped the glasses when I was
bird watching.

Richard anxiously looks around behind him

Richard And you're sure they aren't trailing you?
Nathan Yes! Aren't you proud of me?
Richard Yeah, sure I'm proud of you.

Nathan moves to touch him. Richard snaps

(*Enraged*) Jesus! You and those stupid glasses! You ruined the whole thing, Nathan. You are *not* superior!
Nathan (*shocked*) What do you mean? Yesterday, I thought everything was fine. Yesterday you were helping me ...
Richard I had to protect myself. But, the police aren't gonna let up on you. I can't get into trouble, Nathan.
Nathan The papers say they're checking *several* leads.

Richard, getting more and more angry and scared, grabs Nathan by the collar and shakes him

Richard Goddamn it, that's just cop bullshit. They have nothing except for your "fancy-rich-kid's-gotta-have-special-glasses" — five feet from the body! Your story'll only keep them off for a few days at most. (*He lets him go*)
Nathan (*frightened*) If they suspected me I would be in jail this second.
Richard Did they give you your glasses back?
Nathan No ... they said they needed them.
Richard Then they still think they're evidence! You are so stupid! And not only because of the glasses, you must not have shoved the kid far enough up the pipe or he never would have been found!
Nathan (*exasperated*) I did *exactly* what you told me to do!
Richard You couldn't have!

Nathan desperately tries to calm him

Nathan There's nothing to worry about. Now let's go back to my house.
Richard I'm not going to be within a million miles of you ever again.
Nathan What are you talking about? What about our contract?
Richard (*furious*) I couldn't have foreseen anything like this, Nathan. And I'm not going to have my law career ruined because of you. The cops are gonna start watching every move you make.
Nathan No they won't!
Richard (*finally screaming*) I can't take that chance. I didn't drop *my* glasses.

Richard pushes Nathan violently to the ground and turns to leave. Nathan yells to stop him

Nathan Richard!

Richard turns back to him

I'll go to the police!
Richard (*mocking him*) Right. You'll "go to the police." (*He starts to leave*) I'm leaving and I'm never coming back.
Nathan How could you do this to me?

Richard clenches his fist and moves in for a final threat, causing Nathan to recoil in fear

Richard Fucking idiot.

Richard exits

Music begins. Nathan gets up, brushes himself off, and sings

No. 18 Reprise: Way Too Far

Nathan   How did it come to this?
                         Is something wrong inside me?
                         How did it come to this?
                         It's impossible to run away
                         Or let my conscience guide me.

The Lights change. Nathan faces the parole board

Nathan I was serious. I went straight to the cops. I knew Richard would think I was a low-life, a snitch … a rat. But I didn't care. The next time I saw him was at the police station. I sat there watching as they led him into the holding room with me …

The Lights change for Scene 15

Scene 15

A police interrogation room. Early the next morning

Nathan sits alone in the interrogation room

After a moment, Richard enters. At first confused, he turns and sees Nathan. His blood runs cold

Richard Low-life. Snitch. Rat! You know I can talk my way out of here in minutes.

Nathan Can you?

Richard At least you have the satisfaction of knowing that they picked me up in front of my whole neighbourhood. But I'll get so much sympathy when my "story" comes out. I think I'll give the *Tribune* an exclusive. About how you got me drunk and seduced me ...

Nathan You're going away for a long time.

Richard One of us is. You.

Nathan works up his courage and finally speaks

Nathan Richard ... they cut me a deal. In exchange for you.

Richard What are you talking about? They'd never do that. They only have *your* glasses ...

Nathan They have it all. Every time you told me to wipe something clean or get rid of it — I didn't do it. I kept a drawer full of souvenirs. Like the acid bottle and the crowbar with your fingerprints on them. Our signed contract. I even told them exactly where to find your typewriter — I wonder if they'll be able to match the dropped "Cs" and the faint "Ts" to the ransom note? What would Nietzsche say to that?

Richard stays silent for a moment

Richard So, tell me, will they let you watch me swing? Will it thrill you?

Nathan No.

Richard (*raging at him*) You swore you'd never betray me.

Nathan (*raging back*) You asshole! That's exactly what you were going to do to me!

Richard I wouldn't have gone through with it. But you had no problem selling me out!

Nathan You would have lied to save yourself. At least I "sold you out" with the truth!

Richard You're such a … fucking … lawyer!

Ominous music creeps in

Nathan It's a good deal. I get a few years of easy time, then probation.
   You'll have a different outcome.
Richard No, it's not too late. There's still a way for us to be together …

Music intensifies

No. 19 Keep Your Deal With Me

Richard sings

> So they let you cop a plea, Babe
> I completely empathize!
> But there's still your deal with *me*, Babe
> Can't I please apologize?
> Our chance of freedom's scant
> I assume you won't recant!

Richard slowly approaches Nathan who tries to remain unwavering

> Blood's a lifetime guarantee, Babe!
> Binding contract, no excuse
> Screw the state and stay with me, Babe!
> You don't have to cut me loose!
> Our perfect plan was blown.
> Please don't let me be alone!
> I can sense the way you feel, Babe
> I was wrong before, I know.
> Brought you into this ordeal, Babe
> I don't want to let you go …

As the music swells, Richard takes Nathan's face into his hands and passionately kisses him like his life depends on it. Nathan melts. After a bit, he pulls back, but still holds Richard's hands tightly

Nathan   I'll do what you want me to.
                    There's no me if there's no you!

Music continues

Richard (*speaking*) You'll tell the District Attorney no deal?

Nathan No deal. We're gonna hang together. You know that.
Richard No way. Your father'll spring for the best lawyer money can buy. Won't he?
Nathan I hope so.
Richard Just be strong, like me.

Nathan (*singing*) If we live or get the noose —
Richard   We're together, it's a truce!
Both   If you keep your deal with me!

The Lights change. Nathan speaks to the parole board

Nathan We were taken straight to the Cook County Jail. Richard was in a cell right next to mine. During the days he put up a brave front. But at night, he could never sleep, I would hear him pacing, talking to himself. The last night we were there was the night before the penalty verdict … He didn't know that I couldn't sleep either. I heard everything …

The Lights change for Scene 16

Scene 16

Richard's jail cell. A few months later

As the music pulses, Richard sits tensely in his cell. Nathan feigns sleep in an adjoining cell, which is defined by lighting. Finally Richard gets up and calls quietly over to Nathan

Richard Nathan … Nathan, are you awake?

When he's certain he won't be heard, Richard sings

No. 20 Afraid

I'm afraid to die.
But I'll be damned
If I'll let you know,
You'll never witness me cry!

I'm afraid of court.
Even though the great
Clarence Darrow's behind us,
He may come up short.

Was it wrong to plead?
Saying that we're guilty
Saves taxpayers;
Doesn't save us!
Why concede?

Did we play it right?
I'm afraid of ... fright!

I'm afraid of locks.
I'm afraid of stripes
And of bars
And of being alone in a box!
I can't let you see.
If I show a slight touch of weakness
You'd change your opinion of me!
I'll be sure I'm strong
Even as the judge
Holds my life in his hands
And decides if it's long!

How did I get here?
I'm afraid of ... fear!

When we're punished
If we're sentenced to death
Will that punishment be right?
If we're locked up for life
We can't do it again!
I'm sure they hear that
From a whole lot of men
Who are also unable to
Sleep at night!

I'm afraid to swing
I can feel the noose
Start to tighten,
The pain and the terrible sting!

What we did was wrong
But it seemed right
At the time,
Seemed unreal,
But was real all along.

Everything is black!
But no matter
What they may do to us
Nothing will bring that boy back!

Darrow's gonna try ...
He had *better* try ...
I'm afraid to live ...
I'm afraid to die!

The Lights change. Nathan addresses the parole board

Nathan Waiting for the Judge's decision was torture — after weeks
of uninterrupted agony. But all of a sudden, it was over. And they
chained us up, put us in the back of a wagon, and drove us away ...

The Lights change for Scene 17

Scene 17

The back of a prison transportation wagon

*Nathan and Richard, with their arms behind their backs (as if shackled)
sit silently riding to prison. Their faces are only illuminated by the lights
of the oncoming cars. Finally Nathan speaks*

Nathan Are you afraid?
Richard Of Joliet? I'm not afraid of anything. Of course, I'm a little
worried that my father may organize a lynch mob. How about you?
Nathan I guess I'm just nervous.
Richard Don't be. I thought for sure they'd hang us!
Nathan A penalty trial with no jury. I thought we'd be done for.
Richard But Darrow's speech, arguing against "an eye for an eye" ...
literature! I thought even Bobby Frank's folks bought into it!
Nathan What a summation.
Richard You know what?
Nathan What?
Richard He's exactly the kind of lawyer I'm going to be.

Nathan looks at him with astonishment, then changes his demeanour

Nathan I've got a surprise.

Richard Yeah?

Nathan Once the heat from the press cools down, we're gonna be put in the same cell.

Richard What the hell are you talking about? They'll never put the "thrill-killers" together.

Nathan Prison officials can be bribed, you know.

Richard You can't be serious.

Nathan Dead serious. We're gonna spend the rest of our lives in a cage together like two rare birds. Now you'll never be able to leave me.

Richard (*shocked*) You're nuts.

Nathan (*pleased with himself*) No. I'm a superior human being.

Richard What?

Music begins

Nathan I'm superior to *you*. After all, I stayed one step ahead of you.

Richard What do you mean "ahead"? You followed me ... all the way here.

Nathan Is that what you think? It's funny how the whole world keeps saying the murder had no reason. Because it did have a reason. For me to have you all to myself. Even in prison. You know that's what I've always wanted.

Richard (*almost frightened*) But, you dropped your glasses ... otherwise we never would have ...

Nathan Don't you get it? I dropped them on purpose.

Richard You wanted to get caught?!

Nathan Yes.

Music intensifies. Richard lets it all sink in as Nathan, eerily content, sings

No. 21 Life Plus Ninety-Nine Years

You thought that you used me.
And thought you confused me!
So I did what
Wasn't expected.
You never suspected
And now ...

We'll be together
For life —
Plus ninety-nine years!

I'll keep you focused,
No outside forces!
For life plus ninety-nine years.
Who's in control now?
Who's got resources,
Once the smoke clears?
Not forever
But for life plus ninety-nine years!
Life plus ninety-nine years ...

Music continues

Richard But ... I talked you out of your deal.
Nathan Exactly like I knew you would.
Richard What if we got the death penalty?
Nathan As long as we were together.
Richard This is crazy.
Nathan Am I scaring you?
Richard You son of a bitch ... (*He sings*)

You finally topped me;
You finally stopped me.
And though I admit I believe you
I swear that I'll leave you again!

Nathan   No, we'll be together for —
Both   Life plus ninety-nine years ...

Nathan   You're looking paler!
Richard   How could you do it?
Both   For life plus ninety-nine years ...

Richard   You've been preparing ...
                 I can't go through it!

Nathan   Spare me the tears!

Both   Not forever —
                 But for life plus ninety-nine years ...
                 For life plus ninety-nine years ...
                 Life plus ninety-nine years!

Richard   Life plus ninety-nine ...
Nathan   Life plus ninety-nine years.

*The music continues as the Lights change and Nathan returns to the
parole board*

EPILOGUE

Parole board hearing room. 1958

*Nathan puts his prison uniform back on and once again sits before the
parole board*

Parole Board Voice 2 You deliberately left a clue at the scene? Have
you at last provided us with the final piece of the puzzle?

Nathan I told you ... I just did it to be with Richard. It was the only way
I could justify the ... you know ... knowing we'd be punished.

Parole Board Voice 1 Regardless, you cannot be granted parole until
you show true remorse. Mr Leopold, do you accept what you did and
have remorse for your crime?

Nathan (*sincerely*) Yes I do. Almost every day I think about what we
did to that poor little boy. I wish it never happened.

Parole Board Voice 1 What about Richard Loeb? How do you think
of him today?

Nathan I think if he wasn't stabbed to death in the shower room so
many years ago, I'd have probably ... well ... I don't suppose I should
say that.

Parole Board Voice 2 He's someone you never should have gotten
involved with. Then your life may have been different. Don't you
agree?

Nathan Yes. But if you finally grant me parole, my life can be different.

Parole Board Voice 1 Until we received this letter, from former District
Attorney Crowe, we hadn't reached a decision.

Nathan My prosecutor?

Parole Board Voice 1 He wanted you to hang and still believes you
should have. But since you didn't, he doesn't feel the taxpayers should
be responsible for you any more —

Nathan New killers like me every day? And lawyers to spare them from
the death penalty?

Parole Board Voice 2 (*interrupting*) Truthfully, we need the beds.

Parole Board Voice 1 Therefore, Mr Leopold, it is the decision of this
board to grant your petition for parole.

Parole Board Voice 2 You're a free man.

Nathan, in shock, stands

Nathan Free ... free?
Parole Board Voice 1 This parole hearing is over.

The gavel is struck. The music stops

Parole Board Voice 2 Your things will be returned to you upon your release tomorrow morning.

The Lights begin to narrowly focus in on Nathan's face as the music begins again

Nathan My things? Seventy-four dollars and twelve cents ... my solid gold pocket-watch ... a pack of "Luckies" that must be awfully stale after 34 years ... and a picture taken in nineteen eighteen in Jackson Park ... of Richard. (*He looks off into the darkness, and mutters to himself*) Richard ...

In a ghostly, hazy light, Richard appears, casually smoking a cigarette. He looks to Nathan

Richard (*warmly*) Babe.

Nathan sings to him

No. 22 Thrill Me Finale

Nathan   I'm one perfect accomplice
                     Who'd never betray you —

As Richard blows a long stream of smoke into the air, the light on him fades, causing him to slowly disappear

                     If you thrill me ...

All alone, Nathan softly sings his final words

                     Thrill me! (*He smiles*)

Black-out. (*First applause break*)

CURTAIN

FURNITURE AND PROPERTY LIST

On stage: Black cubes, crates, platforms, or other multi-use pieces

Scene 1

Set: Pair of binoculars (for **Nathan**)

Personal: **Nathan**: pocket-watch, cigarette lighter
    Richard: cigarette case containing cigarettes

Scene 2

Strike: Binoculars

Set: Can of gasoline

Scene 3

Strike: Can of gasoline

Set: Nietzsche book
    Portable Underwood typewriter containing sheet of paper

Personal: **Nathan**: reading glasses (in pocket)
    Richard: sharp-looking pocket knife (in pocket)

Scene 4

Strike: Nietzsche book
    Typewriter

Off stage: Bag full of stolen loot containing silver tray, candlesticks
    etc. (**Nathan** and **Richard**)

Scene 5

On stage: As before

SCENE 6

Personal: **Richard**: cigarette and lighter

SCENE 7

Strike: Bag full of loot

Set: Rope
Crowbar
Small bottle of acid
Leather case

SCENE 8

Personal: **Richard**: cigarette case, 1920s-style car ignition key (in pocket)

SCENE 9

Off stage: Blood-stained rag, crowbar, rope and empty bottle of
acid (**Richard**)
Blood-stained rag, empty leather case (**Nathan**)

SCENE 10

Strike: Rags, crowbar, rope, bottle of acid, leather case

Set: Underwood typewriter containing sheet of paper

SCENE 11

Strike: Typewriter

Set: Two candlestick-style telephones

SCENE 12

Strike: Telephones

SCENE 13

On stage: As before

SCENE 14

On stage: As before

SCENE 15

On stage: As before

SCENE 16

On stage: As before

SCENE 17

On stage: As before

EPILOGUE

Off stage: Lit cigarette (**Richard**)

LIGHTING PLOT

PROLOGUE

To open: Darkness

| Cue 1 | Prelude music begins | (Page 1) |
| | *Lights slowly fade up* | |

| Cue 2 | **Nathan** removes his prison uniform and cap | (Page 3) |
| | *Lights become brighter for* SCENE 1 | |

SCENE 1

To open: Bright exterior lighting

| Cue 3 | **Nathan**: "But not the way that I do!" | (Page 8) |
| | *Lights change to parole hearing board room* | |

| Cue 4 | **Nathan**: "... they always lit on the first strike ..." | (Page 8) |
| | *Lights change for* SCENE 2 | |

SCENE 2

To open: Dim glow from the burning warehouse on **Nathan** and **Richard**

| Cue 5 | **Nathan** throws a splash of gasoline into the distance | (Page 8) |
| | *Immense flames illuminate* **Nathan** *and* **Richard** *fully* | |

| Cue 6 | **Richard** and **Nathan** get intimate | (Page 10) |
| | *Glow of fire grows bigger, brighter and hotter and finally fades. Lights change back to parole hearing board room* | |

| Cue 7 | **Nathan**: "... real late that night ..." | (Page 10) |
| | *Lights change for* SCENE 3 | |

SCENE 3

To open: Interior lighting for **Richard**'s bedroom, night

Cue 8	**Richard** snaps his knife shut	(Page 17)
	Lights change to parole hearing board room	
Cue 9	**Nathan**: "... I noticed a change ..."	(Page 17)
	Lights change for SCENE 4	

SCENE 4

To open: Interior lighting for **Nathan**'s bedroom

Cue 10	**Nathan** reaches for **Richard**	(Page 20)
	Lights shift to parole hearing board room for SCENE 5	

SCENE 5

To open: Interior lighting for parole board hearing room

Cue 11	**Nathan**: "... about five minutes later ..."	(Page 21)
	Lights change for SCENE 6	

SCENE 6

To open: Interior lighting for **Nathan**'s bedroom

Cue 11	**Richard**: "Better than my brother John!"	(Page 24)
	Lights change to parole hearing board room	
Cue 12	**Nathan**: "Richard needed three days to get ready."	(Page 24)
	Lights change for SCENE 7	

SCENE 7

To open: Interior lighting for **Richard**'s garage, on **Richard**'s side of the stage

Cue 13	**Richard**: "It's *not* the kind I told you to get."	(Page 25)
	Crossfade to parole hearing board room on **Nathan**'s *side of the stage*	
Cue 14	**Nathan**: "Much too late to start resisting."	(Page 25)
	Crossfade to garage on **Richard**'s *side of the stage*	
Cue 15	**Richard**: "The crowbar, however, is per-fect-o."	(Page 25)
	Crossfade to parole hearing board room on **Nathan**'s *side of the stage*	
Cue 16	**Nathan**: "Or let my conscience guide me."	(Page 25)
	Crossfade to garage on **Richard**'s *side of the stage*	

Cue 17   **Richard**: "... have to find a damned small boy."   (Page 26)
               Crossfade to parole hearing board room on **Nathan***'s side of the stage*

Cue 18   **Nathan**: "But had no use in fighting."   (Page 26)
               Crossfade to garage on **Richard's** *side of the stage*

Cue 19   **Richard** exits   (Page 26)
               Crossfade to parole hearing board room on **Nathan***'s side of the stage*

Cue 20   **Nathan**: "Then I let it go too far."   (Page 26)
               Lights change for SCENE 8

SCENE 8

To open: Glowing headlights illuminate **Richard**

Cue 21   **Nathan** exits   (Page 28)
               Lights fade to near black, then change for SCENE 9

SCENE 9

To open: Exterior lighting for woods at night

Cue 22   **Nathan**: "This has gone way too far!"   (Page 31)
               Lights change to parole board hearing room

Cue 23   **Nathan**: "... he got out the Underwood ..."   (Page 31)
               Lights change for SCENE 10

SCENE 10

To open: Interior lighting for **Richard**'s bedroom

Cue 24   **Nathan** takes the note from **Richard**   (Page 34)
               Lights change for SCENE 11

SCENE 11

To open: Virtual darkness

Cue 25   Radio broadcast fades out   (Page 34)
               Isolated light on **Nathan**

Cue 26   **Nathan**: "Very important."   (Page 34)
               Isolated light on **Richard**

Cue 27   **Nathan** and **Richard** hang up   (Page 35)
                Lights change to reflect the passage of time

Cue 28   **Nathan** and **Richard** hang up   (Page 36)
                Lights change to reflect the passage of time

Cue 29   **Nathan** and **Richard** hang up   (Page 38)
                Lights change for SCENE 12

SCENE 12

To open: Interior lighting for parole board hearing room

Cue 30   **Nathan**: " ... how fast they found me ..."   (Page 38)
                Lights change for SCENE 13

SCENE 13

To open: Interior lighting for **Nathan**'s bedroom

Cue 31   **Richard** exits   (Page 42)
                Harsh interrogation light on **Nathan**

Cue 32   **Nathan**: "I'm trying to think!" (2nd time)   (Page 42)
                Lights change to parole board hearing room

Cue 33   **Nathan**: "... more than ever ..."   (Page 42)
                Lights change for SCENE 14

SCENE 14

To open: Exterior lighting for Jackson Park, afternoon

Cue 34   **Nathan**: "Or let my conscience guide me."   (Page 44)
                Lights change to parole board hearing room

Cue 35   **Nathan**: "... into the holding room with me ..."   (Page 44)
                Lights change for SCENE 15

SCENE 15

To open: Interior lighting for the police interrogation room, early morning

Cue 36   **Nathan** and **Richard**: "If you keep your deal with me!" (Page 47)
                Lights change to parole board hearing room

Cue 37   **Nathan**: "I heard everything ..."   (Page 47)
                Lights change for SCENE 16

SCENE 16

To open: Interior lighting for **Richard** and **Nathan**'s jail cells

Cue 38   **Richard**: "I'm afraid to die!"   (Page 49)
                  Lights change to parole board hearing room

Cue 39   **Nathan**: "... and drove us away ..."   (Page 49)
                  Lights change for SCENE 17

SCENE 17

To open: Headlights of oncoming cars illuminate **Richard**'s and **Nathan**'s faces

Cue 40   **Nathan**: "Life plus ninety-nine years."   (Page 51)
                  Lights change for EPILOGUE

EPILOGUE

To open: Interior lighting for parole board hearing room

Cue 41   **Parole Board 2**: "... your release tomorrow morning."   (Page 53)
                  Lights narrow in on Nathan's face

Cue 42   **Nathan**: "Richard ..."   (Page 53)
                  Ghostly, hazy light on **Richard** *as he enters*

Cue 43   **Richard** blows a long stream of smoke   (Page 53)
                  Fade light on **Richard**

Cue 44   **Nathan** smiles   (Page 53)
                  Black-out

EFFECTS PLOT

Cue 1   **Nathan** sits   (Page 1)
Parole Board Voice 1 *as script p 1; then the strike*
of a gavel; then **Parole Board Voice 1** *as script p 1*

Cue 2   **Nathan**: "You want the facts again."   (Page 1)
Parole Board Voice 2 *as script pp 1-2, and* **Parole Board**
Voice 1 *as script p 2*

Cue 3   **Nathan**: "That's the truth."   (Page 2)
Parole Board Voice 1 *as script p 2 and* **Parole Board**
Voice 2 *as script p 2*

Cue 4   **Nathan**: "And since."   (Page 2)
Parole Board Voice 1 *as script p 2*

Cue 5   Music for "Why" begins   (Page 2)
Parole Board Voice 2 *as script p 2*

Cue 6   **Nathan** faces the parole board   (Page 20)
Parole Board Voice 1 *as script p 20*

Cue 7   **Nathan**: "I had no choice."   (Page 20)
Parole Board Voice 2 *as script p 20*

Cue 8   **Nathan**: "... I would do whatever he asked."   (Page 20)
Parole Board Voice 1 *as script p 20*

Cue 9   **Nathan**: "... how my conscience worked then."   (Page 20)
Parole Board Voice 2 *as script p 20*

Cue 10   To open SCENE 8   (Page 27)
Billows of exhaust

Cue 11   To open SCENE 11   (Page 34)
Sound of static; then **Radio Newscaster Voice** *as script*
p 34; then fades

Cue 12   Lights change   (Page 35)
Radio Newscaster Voice *as script p 35*

Cue 13	Lights change **Radio Newscaster Voice** *as script p 36*	(Page 36)
Cue 14	**Nathan** stands in front of the parole board **Parole Board Voice 1** *as script p 38*	(Page 38)
Cue 15	**Nathan:** "It didn't seem important." **Parole Board Voice 2** *as script p 38*	(Page 38)
Cue 16	**Nathan:** "It didn't seem important." **Parole Board Voice 2** *as script p 38 and* **Parole Board Voice 1** *as script p 38*	(Page 38)
Cue 17	**Nathan:** "That's not how I would characterize it." **Parole Board Voice 1** *as script p 38*	(Page 38)
Cue 18	**Nathan** sits before the parole board **Parole Board Voice 2** *as script p 52*	(Page 52)
Cue 19	**Nathan:** "... knowing we'd be punished." **Parole Board Voice 1** *as script p 52*	(Page 52)
Cue 20	**Nathan:** "I wish it never happened." **Parole Board Voice 1** *as script p 52*	(Page 52)
Cue 21	**Nathan:** "... I don't suppose I should say that." **Parole Board Voice 2** *as script p 52*	(Page 52)
Cue 22	**Nathan:** "... my life can be different." **Parole Board Voice 1** *as script p 52*	(Page 52)
Cue 23	**Nathan:** "My prosecutor?" **Parole Board Voice 1** *as script p 52*	(Page 52)
Cue 24	**Nathan:** "... spare them from the death penalty?" **Parole Board Voice 2** *as script p 52 and* **Parole Board voice 1** *as script p 52*	(Page 52)
Cue 25	**Nathan:** "Free ... free?" **Parole Board Voice 1** *as script p 53; then gavel is struck; then* **Parole Board Voice 2** *as script p 53*	(Page 53)